SALES RULES!
24 Sales Strategies for Becoming the Best

David B Dykstra

© 2018 David B Dykstra
All rights reserved.

Published by Double D Publishing
Comstock Park, MI 49321
www.DoubleD.pub

Visit the Author's website at *www.DavidBDykstra.com*

Sales Rules!

Bend the rules if you must. Don't break them..................................7
Rule 1 - Never Cheat your Customer 9
Rule 2 - You Learn to Win by Losing...11
Rule 3 - Never Be Unreachable 15
Rule 4 - Never Assume...17
Rule 5 - Don't Worry about Credit 19
Rule 6 - Never, Ever Beg 21
Rule 7 - Don't Hold on Too Tight...23
Rule 8 - Opportunities are Everywhere 25
Rule 9 - Never, Ever Quit 27
Rule 10 - One Question, One Minute 29
Rule 11 - Stop Selling and Let Them Buy 31
Rule 12 - Tell the Truth 33
Rule 13 - Look Beyond the Obvious...35
Rule 14 - Attitude Matters 37
Rule 15 - Don't Break Their Trust...39
Rule 16 - Follow Up 41
Rule 17 - Tell the Story 43
Rule 18 - If You Need Help, Ask 45
Rule 19 - Make Them Love You 47
Rule 20 - When You Sell It, Stop Selling 49
Rule 21 - Not Everything is a Nail 51
Rule 22 - You Can't Please Everyone 53
Rule 23 - Some Will, Some Won't. Move On..................................55
Rule 24 - Sometimes - You Fail 57
Final Rule – Find a True Companion 59

To Kathryn - My Friend, My Hero, My True Companion

Bend the rules if you must. Don't break them.

"The responsibility of the leader is to teach their people the rules, train them to gain competency and build their trust. At that point, leadership must step back and trust that their people know what they are doing and will do what needs to be done." ~ *Simon Sinek*

Leroy Jethro Gibbs is the ultimate federal agent. He has his own code for life and getting things done. He lives the rules discovered from his past experiences, good and bad.

Kathryn and I enjoy watching the CBS crime drama NCIS. Gibbs' main job is to teach the rules to his team. His team learns the rules and lives them, even though they may not understand them. The rules are important for their success, both professionally and personally. Should they choose to ignore or break the rules, there will be hell to pay!

From this influence comes *Sales Rules!* After 20+ years of selling and leading sales teams, several rules are critical to my success. I wrote them down and finally decided it was time to share them with you.

I have learned and lived these rules from mentors as well as my own experiences. I present the rules in no particular order. None is more important than another. Plus, in my experience, things never happen in an organized, flow-charted way. A skilled, effective salesperson needs to know the right thing to do.

When you know the rules, you know what's right. Every rule is important in its own way and at its own time. As a strong, confident professional, you know what you need to do. You even know that sometimes, the rules may get in the way of doing the right thing for your customer.

Never break a rule. But, if you must break a rule, know why you are breaking it. Weak people break rules to make things easy for themselves. Strong people never break the rules unless it is the only right thing to do for the benefit of someone else.

Everyone needs their own code for their life. Make notes about each rule and what it means to you. Find the rules that are missing and make them your own. Develop your own list by adding your own rules, but only add a rule when it truly defines you.

The rules are not the secret to closing more deals or finding more prospects. They do make you a better person and a strong, confident leader.

Some of these rules are easy to understand (*Tell the Truth*), and some are much harder. But this is my guarantee: if you start learning and using these rules today, you will become better.

Sales is simple, but it is rarely easy. It will take your entire career before you feel like you got it right. But remember, *You Learn to Win by Losing*. And *Never, Ever Quit*!

Rule 1 - Never Cheat your Customer

"You must never actually cheat the customer, even if you can. You must make her happy and satisfied, so she will come back." ~ *Alexander Turney Stewart*

Have you ever felt cheated by someone? How did that make you feel? Would you ever do business with them again?

According to the White House Office of Consumer Affairs, a dissatisfied customer tells 10-15 people about their terrible experience. About 1 in 8 of these customers will tell more than 20 people, especially if the issue had a simple resolution. In fact, people who feel wronged are 10 times more likely to tell others than those with good experiences.

In other words, if you give a customer a bad deal, expect others to hear about it. Where I work, we often hear about service issues of our nearest brand competitor. The last thing I want is for my customers to tell them the same thing about me.

96% of unhappy customers don't complain at all; they simply never come back. You can also assume that they are not giving you any amazing referrals. If you want to succeed and grow in sales, you will need both repeat customers and referrals. Why?

1. The probability of selling to an existing customer is 60-70%.
2. The probability of selling to a new customer with a good referral is 40-50%.
3. The probability of selling to a cold prospect is 5-20%.

Without repeat customers and referrals, every sale is difficult and has the least chance of success.

Remember, your reputation (and the reputation of your company) is on the line with every customer. It is very enjoyable when your customer tells you about their friend who loved working with you. Doing damage control with an upset customer is never fun.

Rule 2 - You Learn to Win by Losing

"You can't win unless you learn how to lose." ~ Kareem Abdul-Jabbar

---

No career is more loaded with sports metaphors than sales. "The ball's in their court." "Down to the wire." "Slam dunk!" "Take one for the team." And why not? What other career is more filled with the ideas of competition and victory than sales?

Sales is all about winning, but it is practically defined by losing. Every person who has been in sales more than five minutes knows that you lose more deals than you win. If that is not true, then you are an order taker, not a salesperson.

A successful career in sales demands that you pay your dues. Fortunately, paying your dues is no longer doing busy work or getting lunch for the other sales reps. It's all about learning what it takes to be successful by trying and failing and learning from failure. Getting good takes time, even for the best.

Michael Jordan is one of the greatest basketball players of all time. His NBA career spanned 15 years. Jordan started 1,039 of 1,072 games. His shots-made percentage is 49.7% (51.5% of 2-point shots). His free-throw percentage is 83.5% and his average points per game is over 30. He played in six NBA championships and won all six. And if that's not impressive enough, he scored 32,292 points.

Even with those impressive stats, Michael wasn't perfect. He didn't make the varsity team in high school, he never won an NCAA championship, and he didn't go Number One in the NBA draft. Of his 1,072 professional games, he lost 366. That's quite a record of failure for one of the Greatest ballplayers of All Time!

What does Jordan say about winning and losing?

> "I've missed more than 9,000 shots in my career. I've lost almost 300 games. 26 times, I've been trusted to take the game winning shot and missed. I've failed over and over and over again in my life. And that is why I succeed." (Michael Jordan, 1997)

Losing is a part of the game. No one wins every time, even in the most amazing career. Losing gives you the opportunity to learn from experience. If you consider what went wrong, you can prepare for the next time.

Did you miss something early in the process? Did something change for the customer? Did you miss a sign that the deal was going sideways? Whatever happened, take a few minutes to consider what you can change next time. Most importantly, don't look for a reason to blame someone else.

If you are afraid to fail, you will never come close to reaching your potential. Failure can be the best, most underrated teacher you will ever have. If you never fail, you're not trying hard enough to be better than you currently are.

One more sports quote:

> "Sportsmanship for me is when a guy walks off the court and you really can't tell whether he won or lost, when he carries himself with pride either way." ~ Jim Courier

You will lose. Accept the loss. Keep your head high, step back, and reexamine the deal. Retool and retrain if necessary. Learn from your mistakes and improve yourself.

Then go out and start again.

Rule 3 - Never Be Unreachable

"If you are not taking care of your customer, your competitor will." ~ Bob Hooey

Your customer must be able to reach you when they need you. It may be for the craziest reason and at the worst time, but when your customer needs you, you need to be available. If you aren't available, your competitor is.

Your customer needs multiple ways to reach you. Give them your cell phone, email, Facebook, Twitter, smoke signals, and any other method possible. The more ways you give your customer to reach you, the more secure they will feel about doing business with you.

One warning - if you give a customer a way to reach you, make sure you respond quickly. If you only log into Twitter once a week, don't use it as a reliable contact. If you live on Facebook or your blog, that's a perfect opportunity to be available.

Give your customers options; not every customer will want to communicate the same way. If they don't like phone calls, send them letters. If they don't like receiving direct mail they can opt to receive coupons and reminders through email. Keeping them happy is what keeps them coming back and boosts your sales and your commission.

Communicate good, useful, and correct information. Never stop communicating.

Be ready, willing, and able to be your customer's "go-to" person. It's the little things that make the difference between good, better, and best!

Rule 4 - Never Assume

"Never assume the obvious is true." ~ William Safire

How many times do you know what the customer is going to do, only to discover that they did the exact opposite?

"This deal is done." As a sales manager, I heard that more times than I can count. They knew that the customer was buying. They got the handshake. They got money down. They just needed to finish the paperwork.

And then the prospect pulled a vanishing act. Or, even worse, the signed contract was 'in the mail,' but it never showed up.

Salespeople tend to hear what they want to hear. They struggle to ask the right questions, fearing the answers may not be what they want.

You need to know the real, current status of every deal. Make it an integral part of your sales process. How do you do this? Ask the right questions:

1. Ask them what the next steps are for finishing the sale
2. Ask them to summarize where they are in the process
3. Ask them if they can think of any red flags that might pop up

Watch out for words like "maybe", "probably", or "future." These are non-committal words that could show a lack of commitment.

If your customer is not ready to give you a commitment, be direct. "When you say that you need to check with upper management, who is that? Let's give them a call while I am here so that we can work out any issues together."

Customers never tell you everything. You need to ask the right questions to make sure you have all the information. You don't need to be overbearing, just direct. Sales is about leading, so lead your customer in the process. When you assume the sale, you could lose the sale.

Assuming is dangerous; it's arrogant, it's lazy, and it doesn't work. As a rule, never, ever assume.

Rule 5 - Don't Worry about Credit

"It is amazing what you can accomplish if you do not care who gets the credit." ~ Harry Truman

President Reagan kept a small plaque on his desk in the Oval Office. It said, "There is no limit to what a man can do or where he can go if he does not mind who gets the credit."

Yes, it's true that, in sales, the one who gets the credit is usually the one who gets paid. Credit creates competition that drives people to improve but can also destroy relationships.

When I sold cars, the dealership had a policy that if you sold a customer a car once, they were your customer for life. This policy is good until the customer's salesperson is on vacation or the customer doesn't let you know. You work the customer, find them the right deal, finish everything, and get them out the door in their new car. Only then do you discover that you got nothing for all the work except, if you are lucky, a "Thank You."

I hated that. I even told my sales manager that I wouldn't do it anymore. I was only going to work with people who had not bought before. He didn't argue; he even said he understood.

About two months later, I noticed that I wasn't getting any extra help from my manager. He would only spend time working with me if it was necessary. He wouldn't pass customers to me as often as he used to. This change was frustrating because I thought we had a great relationship. During a review, I noticed that he had taken "helpful" off my list of strengths. He never mentioned it; he accepted my decision and managed me that way. I got the message.

Once I stopped worrying about getting credit, my relationship with my manager improved. My attitude toward the job and my customers improved as well. My sales increased, and I was happier.

Be the one who will do anything for anyone. Customers notice, and so do managers and your peers. Your life is not about one deal; take your eyes off the short game and don't worry about credit. Your change in attitude will pay off.

Rule 6 - Never, Ever Beg

"You will never gain anyone's approval by begging for it. When you stand confident in your own worth, respect follows." ~   Mandy Hale

---

Both sides need to be happy for a deal to work. If you can't make that happen, let it go.

I had a manager who was a champion of this philosophy. When a customer started pushing for a discount, he would tell them our cost. He would then explain that we needed to make a profit and he would show them the profit margin.

He would always finish by saying, "Both sides need to be happy for a deal to work." With this transparency and a great attitude, he usually closed the deal.

Customers understand that you need to make a profit to keep the lights on. They just don't want to feel like they are paying for the entire year's electric bill. When you are upfront, transparent, and honest with them, most customers will find a way to work with you.

You will never gain anyone's approval by begging for it. When you stand confident in your own worth, respect follows. When you beg for a deal, your self-respect suffers, and the customer loses respect for you. If they do come back as a repeat, they will expect the same type of discount, if not a steeper one.

This confidence is a change of mindset. Being desperate cheapens the value of your product or service. It destroys your profit margin and it kills your commission.

If you need to beg someone to buy your product or service, it means one of three things:
1. You don't believe your product is worth the price you are charging
2. You are targeting the wrong audience with your product
3. You were not offering the right product for your customer's needs

If you don't believe your product is not worth the price, you shouldn't be selling it. You must believe that you are giving your customers the best solution for their problem. Otherwise, you are just selling snake oil.

Rule 7 - Don't Hold on Too Tight

"Managing is like holding a dove in your hand. If you hold it too tightly you kill it, but if you hold it too loosely, you lose it." ~ Tommy Lasorda

---

Your life and success are not based on a single customer or a single deal. Release the death grip you have on the deal and let your customer breathe.

If a customer needs time to consider their options, you need to respect them and give them some space. Is it possible that they will buy elsewhere? Yes, but that is possible anyway. Is it possible they will change their mind? Yes, but then was your product or service the best choice for them? Is it possible that they will see your allowance as weakness? I don't think so. They see it as a sign of respect.

Customers are like sand. If you hold sand with an open hand, the sand stays where it is. As soon as you squeeze your hand to hold on, the sand seeps between your fingers and falls to the ground. You may save a bit of it, but most will be gone, slipped from your grasp.

A customer is like that. Held loosely, with respect and consideration for their needs and opinions, they will stay with you. But apply too much pressure, and the customer, like the sand, will fall away and disappear.

I will say it again: respect your customer and their process. There is no long-term benefit for forcing their hand. Any benefit is yours alone, and that's selfish. I have heard so many customers tell me that they left a competitor because they felt pressured to buy. People want time to consider their purchases, and why shouldn't they be able to do that?

Solve your customer's problem with a valid, workable, affordable solution. Present your solution like your life depends on it. Answer the objections. Do your best to close the deal and ask for the sale. If they need time, clarify the deal, and set a follow-up appointment (face to face if possible). But don't try to force your customer into buying.

One deal will never make or break your career. A repeat customer might.

Rule 8 - Opportunities are Everywhere

"The best time to plant a tree was 20 years ago. The second-best time is now." ~ Chinese proverb

---

This rule should be completely obvious to you, but, then, the best rules usually are.

Your business card is one of the most important marketing tools you have. It says who you are, what you do, and how they can find you. It is easy to carry and easy to give away. It can get you a customer or a referral. People keep well-made business cards for current or future reference.

How many times have you scribbled a name and number on a scrap of paper, and then lost it? Why risk it?

Always carry a few business cards. Have several in your car, your desk, and at your home. Never be without them. When someone asks what you do, pull out a card, hand it to them, and continue with your conversation. They may forget everything you say, but they will take your card and put it on their desk or in a drawer. When they need you, they will know how to reach you.

One more thought: give some to your spouse. You never know who they might run into that needs what you offer.

There is never a wrong time to look for the next customer. As I am writing this, I have had two separate customers of a fellow salesman stop in. He has been working with these people for weeks if not months. Today (his day off, of course) they stopped in ready to buy.

Had he waited to introduce himself, he would have missed both deals, because I would have claimed them.

The best time to look for a customer is before they know they want to buy your product.

Rule 9 - Never, Ever Quit

"Never give in--never, never, never, never, in nothing great or small, large or petty, never give in except to convictions of honor and good sense. Never yield to force; never yield to the apparently overwhelming might of the enemy." ~ Winston Churchill

People often say, "When the going gets tough, the tough get going." The going is always tough in sales. If you are selling, you are always running, trying to close the deal and deliver the product on time and on point. And if you aren't selling, then you know that things are even tougher.

One thing is true about a career in sales; it can be hell. Literal hell. Nothing works, nothing is right, you feel alone, and it even feels like your family and friends don't understand. When things go wrong at work, everything goes wrong. It is, quite literally, hell.

That is not the time to quit. That is the time to pick yourself up and work harder than you have ever worked. Push through the darkness, knowing that there is light on the other side, even if you can't see it.

During the darkest hours of World War II when Britain was about to fall to the Germans, Winston Churchill, the Prime Minister of England, said:

"Britain, other nations thought, had drawn a sponge across her slate. But instead our country stood in the gap. There was no flinching and no thought of giving in; and by what seemed almost a miracle to those outside these Islands, though we ourselves never doubted it, we now find ourselves in a position where I say that we can be sure that we have only to persevere to conquer." (Oct. 29, 1941 – Speech to Harrow School)

Britain endured under Churchill. He never quit, so they never quit. As Churchill endured, the country endured. They fought on and finally defeated the German army!

Rule 10 - One Question, One Minute

""The best sales questions have your expertise wrapped into them."
~ Jill Konrath

You have one question and one minute to engage the customer. It doesn't matter if the customer is on the showroom floor, in a retail setting, across the table from you, or on the phone. The only way to engage your customer is to ask a question. You have only one minute to ask the right question. If they answer, the clock starts over. If they ignore you or dismiss you, the dance is over. Let them walk away.

When does the clock stop running? When they ask you a question. That's when they become engaged, and only then can you start selling them your product or service.

But, you say, what do I ask them? Here is a list of questions to start with. If these don't work (and they won't all work), make up your own. Write them down, try them out. Get rid of the ones that don't work and keep growing the list. Soon, you won't even need to think about asking questions; they will come naturally.

1. Do you have a couple of minutes?
2. What brings you in today?
3. What kind of project are you working on right now?
4. Is (solution) important to your company?
5. What's more important to you ('A' benefit) or ('B' benefit)?
6. Are you looking for (shoes) or (socks) today?
7. Do you prefer (blue) or (yellow)?
8. What are you trying to get (this devices/tool) to do?

9. Who are you buying this (gift/present/item) for?
10. Are you the only one who will use this (item)?
11. Will you be using this (item) at home or in the car?
12. How will (product or service) most help you?
13. What are your priorities?
14. Are you looking more for savings or durability?
15. Are you planning to do some travelling?
16. Do you need a backup?
17. How'd you hear about us?
18. Is this your first visit?
19. Are you just starting out (with this product/service)?
20. Have you used one of these (items) before?
21. What are your concerns?
22. What alternatives have you looked at?
23. What is your desired outcome?
24. How long do you plan to use this (item/service)?
25. Have you been using (competing product/service)?
26. Are you familiar with this (technology/service)?
27. Are you happy with your current (provider/product/service)?

One Minute. One Question. Make that first question count. Don't blow it on "Can I help you?"

Rule 11 - Stop Selling and Let Them Buy

"Stop selling. Start helping." ~ Zig Ziglar

People don't want to be sold; they want to buy.

Many people think sales is all about pressure and tactics and manipulation. Salespeople can fall into this trap too, especially when the pressure is on to reach your quota.

People don't like "being sold." They hate the lies, manipulation, and pressure that many have come to expect from a sales person. Instead, they want to buy in their own time and using their own criteria. They want the freedom to buy what they want (or need) without feeling ripped off. They want, and deserve, to have control.

What do our sales managers demand? "Get control of your customer!" "Get control of the deal." The truth is that the customer is in total control. They can walk away or dismiss you at any time. But, as salespeople, we need to hold on and sell a little harder. One more question, one more tactic, and I'm sure they will sign the contract. Right?

Wrong.

The outcome of the process is not up to you. The customer holds all the power to purchase. We need to get out of the customer's way and realize that helping our customer find their solution is our only goal, even if the solution is not one we offer.

Our job is to find the solution to the customer's problem and then, if possible, fill their need with something that falls within our line of products or services. The only thing we have control over is presenting our product or service, answering their questions, and making it easy to buy from you. Then, let the customer make up his own mind.

"Make your product easier to buy than your competition, or you will find your customers buying from them, not you." ~ Mark Cuban

The customer controls the decision to buy. You know you can solve their problem. Your success begins when you make it easy for them to buy your solution.

Rule 12 - Tell the Truth

"Honesty is more than not lying. It is truth telling, truth speaking, truth living, and truth loving." ~ James E. Faust

---

Never, never, NEVER lie to a customer.

Telling the truth does three things. First, it makes you feel good. You know at the end of the day you did your best to do your job well.

Second, telling the truth is the only authentic way to earn your customer's trust and respect. Earning someone's trust takes time; a lie wipes out any trust that may have already developed between you. Your customers aren't stupid. They can tell if you are misleading them. Treat them with all the respect that you would want, and they deserve.

Also, remember that it's a small world and people talk. You don't know who your customer knows or what they might say about you, your service, their deal, etc.

Third, telling the truth is liberating! When you are honest with everyone, you never need to remember what "story" you told each person. If you don't tell the truth, it is easy to slip up and say the wrong thing to the wrong person at the wrong time.

Misleading someone into a sale is not satisfying. Lying to your customer is not worth the effort it takes. If you tell the truth, you never need to worry that you changed your tune at the worst possible time.

Successful salespeople have one important thing in common: honesty. Honest communication is important for gaining customers, increasing sales, and getting great referrals.

Sales is not a short game. It takes time, energy, planning, and strategy to win, and honesty must be a major part of that strategy.

What's the "secret" to creating and maintaining credibility with your clients?

Don't lie. *Ever.* End of discussion.

Rule 13 - Look Beyond the Obvious

"What we see depends mainly on what we look for." ~ John Lubbock

---

Don't assume you know what your customer is thinking, even if they are saying all the right words. Before you can propose a solution, you need to be clear on the problem.

A customer was looking at the beautiful pickup in the showroom. I approached him and said something like, "That's a beautiful truck, isn't it?"

"Yeah. Looks like it has everything on it," He replied.

We talked, and I answered every question about all the features, including how much it could haul. We even testing the rear seats. He was in love with this truck, and I knew he wanted it.

After about 20 minutes, I asked if he would be trading anything for his new truck. He looked puzzled, then said, "No, my wife is replacing her car. I don't need a truck." That's when he showed me that she was already working with another sales person.

I fell into the trap. I assumed he was shopping for a truck because he was looking at a truck. I asked leading questions that showed he wanted a truck. Never did he mention that he wasn't in the market for a truck.

But then again, I didn't ask.

You, as the salesperson, are the expert. Our expertise makes us feel like we already know all the answers. But sometimes we forget to (or are afraid to) ask the questions that help us discover what the customer needs.

You can't be the expert if you don't know what the customer needs. When you understand what your customer wants or needs, you stop being pushy and you start solving their problem. You become the expert they need, helping them find exactly what they want, not what you want to sell them.

Rule 14 - Attitude Matters

"Things turn out best for the people who make the best of the way things turn out." ~ John Wooden

---

Attitude is the lifeblood of the salesperson. A great attitude draws people, while a poor attitude drives them away. A bad attitude also pollutes everything you do and say.

Nobody wants to be a part of your pity party. In business, especially in sales, it is critical to keep a negative attitude from taking over our day. Problems are a part of life, and failure is practically a definition of sales. Sometimes we need to fake it; we need to dust ourselves off and move forward.

We all know positive people, don't we? We gravitate toward them and we enjoy their company. When they are around it seems like a cool breeze is blowing, clearing the air, and making life fun again. On the flip side, we know that one person who is always complaining, has a permanent scowl, and sucks the life out of a room. We can predict what they are going to say before they say it because it's always the same and it's always negative.

Which person would you rather be around? Be honest, which one are you?

I once had a coworker who was quite good at selling. He could connect with customers, make friends, and sell without pushing. He was quite successful.

However, whenever a deal went south, it was all he could talk about! Never mind the fact that he was remarkably successful - he continued to dwell on the "NO" and forget about the "YES!"

In Numbers 14:11, we read that the nation of Israel was on the doorstep of their promised land, but they started complaining. Their complaining showed a lack of gratitude to what God had done for them, and it caused God to send Israel into the wilderness for the next 40 years.

Others wish they had your problems. Remember that your attitude defines your next step. If you do not keep your attitude in check, no one will want to be around you. Sales is already a lonely career. Don't drive everyone away.

Complaining drives out gratitude. Complaining shows a lack of trust in what will happen for you and to you.

Guard your heart. Protect your attitude by refusing to complain about your circumstances. Everything flows from your heart into your life, so guard your heart so that you move into the best life has to offer.

Do the next right thing; keep your complaints to yourself.

Rule 15 - Don't Break Their Trust

"Respect is earned, Honesty is appreciated. Trust is gained. Loyalty is returned." ~ Auliq Ice

---

The trust between a customer and salesperson is the foundation of a successful sale. Once it's gone, it's gone, and you can never get it back.

If customers do not like you or trust you, they will not do business with you. Getting a customer to buy from you is not a game of winning and losing but one of relationship and trust.

"Can I trust you?" is a provocative question to ask. Even more dangerous is "Do you trust me?" People trust you only because of what you do. That's all they know about you. They don't know about your feelings, your sincerity, or your good intentions. They only know what you do.

There are five elements that combine to create trust in what we say and do. Trust is not about feelings or intentions, but action.

1. Motivation: To trust someone, I must know that they have my best interests at heart.
2. Integrity: Without integrity on all sides, it is impossible to work together.
3. Communication: Everyone must communicate often, clearly, openly, and honestly.
4. Acceptance: Acceptance is knowing that others respected you no matter what.

5. Reliability: If someone continues to fall short, misses deadlines, or fails at following through, trust in that person goes away.

Distrust exacts a very heavy price that is often very tough to overcome. A customer's lack of trust can backlash in many ways:

1. Both customers and companies lose sight of what is most important and instead focus on 'covering their backs.'
2. Customers start to focus on the shortcomings of the company, leading to indecision.
3. Communication breaks down and trivial matters become more important.
4. Disagreement and blame become part of the regular conversation.
5. The partnership becomes an "us vs. them" mentality.
6. The extra stuff that your company was willing to give seems to disappear.
7. Anxiety replaces assurance and dampens the relationship.

Without trust, the job drains you emotionally. Who wants to be a part of that type of environment? Would you want to show up every morning?

Develop and maintain the trust between you, your company, and your customer. Once you lose trust, it's gone, and so is your customer.

Rule 16 - Follow Up

"I have a simple philosophy: I follow up as many times as necessary until I get a response. I don't care what the response is as long as I get one." ~ Steli Efti

---

Here are a few crazy sales statistics (from Dartnell Corp.):

1. 48 percent of sales reps quit calling after the first contact
2. 72 percent stop after the second contact
3. 84 percent give up after the third contact
4. 92 percent wave surrender after the fourth contact

Half of the sales people you compete with stop contacting a prospect after the first phone call. Only one sales person in four makes the third call.

Here are two more:
1. Only 8 percent of salespeople make the fifth call
2. Studies show that 80 percent of sales close after that fifth sales call

What does this all mean? 80% of sales are going to only 8% of the sales people out there!

That also means people who would buy your product never get the chance because *you stopped trying!*

Should you follow up? Yes. It's your job. Why wouldn't you? Are you afraid that they might say no? *But what if they say yes?*

How often should you follow up? As often as it takes.

Never stop following up. Stack the odds in your favor – keep calling until they say "No" five times.

Don't take these rejections personally. Stay professional and realize that not everyone is on your time line. Customers don't care if you need one more deal to pay for your vacation, or to cover your next house payment.

This rule hit me in the face this past week. This would be my sixth call to this prospect in four months. His budget was the issue. He had told me he didn't think they were a good fit. And he told me that he didn't think his boss would approve of the transaction.

In my mind, I wanted to mark him off my call list. Move on to the next one. In my mind, this was going to be a wasted call.

I called and got a busy signal. That's odd in a world of voice mail and auto attendants. So, I called again because busy signals don't count in my daily call numbers. Another busy signal. I sent him a "Sorry I Missed You" email and prepared to move on.

Something told me to try once more. I hit redial and it rang. I asked for Tommy and he answered right away. I introduced myself and stammered an apology for the email I had just sent. He laughed and said, "We have talked a few times (he remembered me!) and I remember telling you that I didn't think we are a good fit. But I admire your persistence. I want to give you a shot."

Never stop calling. You never know if they were thinking about you and what you offer. They may have lost your contact information. It's not their job to call you - *it's your job to call them.*

If you're always leaving voice mails or messages at the front desk, don't call at the same time on the same day of the week. Don't make the stop so that you can mark off a line on your call sheet.

Be memorable. Do your best every single time. Never stop trying.

Rule 17 - Tell the Story

"There is no sale without the story; no knockout without the setup."
~ Gary Vaynerchuck

There's a saying in the world of sales - "Facts tell, but stories sell." The meaning behind this saying is obvious. If you want a person to buy your products or services, tell them a story.

Facts tell, but a relevant story connects with the customer. It resonates. When it resonates, it becomes a part of them. And when it becomes a part of them, it pushes the process forward.

Your story should lead your customer to your solution without pulling them. Don't preach, just tell the story. The listener will figure things out for themselves.

Your story does not need to be about you. Tell the story of your customers, their problems, your solutions, and their experiences. Use real people, real places, real names (if you have permission).

When I am selling, I am always telling a story. The facts don't make it true. But if I tell you a story about John at Smith Industries in Jacksonville, Florida, and how our system helped them, you begin to understand. And it should be believable, because it's completely true, every word.

I didn't say that John is our best customer (he's not) or that we solved every problem (we didn't). I didn't say that we were the most amazing thing since pockets (we definitely aren't). Story-telling is not the place for hyperbole. You don't need it. Tell the real story and let the customer connect the dots.

Stories connect because they have emotion. Sometimes they are funny, or sad, or touching, or exciting. They should affect the listener in some way or they become forgettable. I know that my stories are effective because they affect me every time I tell them. I laugh, or I become emotional, or I talk faster. These are real emotions on my part, not fake, not manipulative.

Story telling is a lost art that needs to come back, especially in sales. Even when you know the facts, it takes skill and practice to tell a good story. Anybody can recite a set of facts or rattle of statistics or figures and read a PowerPoint slide. This will not surprise anyone. And it won't catch anyone's attention.

Do you want your customer to buy your product? Surprise them with your story; it may surprise you how well it works.

Rule 18 - If You Need Help, Ask

"If you need help, ask for it. Someone will help you. If you're doing good look around because there's probably someone who needs help and you can give it." ~ Larry Morrisey

No one knows everything. You don't need to be the smartest; be the one who can find the answer fastest.

Help is one of those four-letter-words that is curiously difficult to say when it's in the form of a request. Most people tell me that it's not easy for them to ask for help.

Asking for help comes with many challenges. Sometimes we are too proud to ask. Other times, we feel like we are asking others to help us pick up the pieces of our life. Help is a big and powerful word that we should only use as a last resort, right?

Help is a call for a partner, a co-pilot, a friend. I have been with people who did not ask for help. Following the disaster that happened, they asked, "Couldn't you see I needed help?"

That question that follows, of course is, "Why didn't you ask?" We've all been there: waiting for rescue without ask for it. Sigh.

Don't wait until you need help to prepare to need help. Find a mentor or a friend that you can call whenever you need them. They don't even need to be someone in sales or in your industry. They need to be ready and willing.

My best helper is my wife. Kathryn is not in sales; she is a corporate accountant, and she often reminds me that she hates selling. She cringes when I tell her stories of working hard to close a deal, and she thinks I am often pushier than I need to be.

Kathryn is also my hero. She listens while I tell her about problem I am having. She can rarely solve the problem, but she can ask questions and help me find the solution. She encourages me and pushes me beyond what I think I can do. She reminds me that my worth is not dependent on this one deal. Most importantly, she never gives up on me and never lets me give up on myself.

That's the power of two. A second voice, another set of eyes, someone outside of the box in which you have painted yourself.

Find someone who can stand beside you when you need them and is willing to hold you up when you are ready to fall. Even Moses, God's chosen rescuer for the Nation of Israel, had helpers who stood beside him and held his arms up when he was too tired to go on (Exodus 17:8-13).

Don't underestimate the willingness of others to help you. Ask.

Rule 19 - Make Them Love You

"We elect and buy from people we like. Likability is number one. We also need to believe they are honest and have our best interests at heart." ~ George Farris

---

All selling is about the relationship, so make your prospects fall in love with you!

Think about it. Would you rather do business with someone you know or someone you like? And would you be more inclined to trust someone you like or some you love?

How do you make someone fall in love with you? Value them, treat them right, talk to them about things other than your product, and laugh with them. Nothing creates a lasting relationship faster than laughing with someone.

During a particularly long, drawn out week, I was calling prospects in Alabama. Near the end of the day, I made a call and the greeting had a very Midwestern accent. Without thinking, I started to laugh. Then I said, "I'm sorry, but you are not from Alabama, are you."

"No," she replied. "I'm from Ohio. Why?"

I shared with her that I have been hearing the soft southern accent all day, and she sounded nothing like that. "You sound like me," I said.

We laughed for a couple of minutes about that and I made my presentation. We agreed that I would call back in a couple of weeks to follow up.

Two weeks and about a thousand calls later, I called back. I did not remember anything about our earlier conversation, but she did.

I told my husband about you after we spoke," she said. "He laughed at me because I don't have an accent."

I felt stupid that I had forgotten the conversation. But she remembered the whole thing. Suddenly, I was not talking to a prospect, but to a friend. She was new in the job and I was the first outsider to make her feel like she could succeed. We offered exactly what she needed, and she now had a friend who could help her.

I will not forget her again. I have a new friend in Alabama. And Ohio. And California. And Texas. It's not about my products or my skill. I made them laugh and we became friends.

Laugh. Get personal. Tell them about your family. And don't do it because it will move the sale along or because it's part of the process. Be genuine. Do it to make a friend. Do it to be a friend.

Do it because it is so much better to go to work with your friends than with a bunch of strangers who don't care about you.

Rule 20 - When You Sell It, Stop Selling

"When you get the answer you want, hang up!" — Brad Pitt as Billy Beane, *"Moneyball"*

The best sales advice I can offer is that once your clients or customers agree to buy from you, stop selling. Period.

No, don't hang up the phone on them. But stop selling.

It doesn't matter what you are selling. As soon as the customer says "yes," say "thank you" and move into getting your many ducks to line up. You want their experience to be amazing and memorable.

Oh, and don't forget to Rocky fist-pump once you hang up the phone!

I have seen terrific sales people shoot themselves in the foot many times. They make the sale, and, because they can't stop, they un-sell the customer. They continue pitching features and benefits, never moving the process along.

The problem could be that they don't know what to do once they get the yes (been there). They know how to pitch, but not what to do next, so they keep pitching.

The problem could also be "yakkity-yak syndrome." This is when people talk nonstop. It's like they need to hear themselves talk. So, they ramble on and on. Like a run-away car on a mountain highway, they keep going until they hit something.

There is a simple two-step solution. First, listen to your customer, not to reply, but to hear and respond to what they say. When the customer is talking, LISTEN! Don't be preparing your next point or trying to decide what close you are going to use. Be present.

Second, when the client agrees to the sale: STOP.

It really is that easy. Don't let nerves, insecurities or even quiet tempt you to keep going. Be prepared to move to the next part of the selling process - Delivery.

Rule 21 - Not Everything is a Nail

"You don't have to know everything as long as you know people who know the things you don't." ~ Harvey Mackay

"If the only tool you have is a hammer, everything looks like a nail."

This is the Law of the Instrument, and Abraham Maslow first said it in 1966. The natural tendency is to depend on the skill set we currently have rather than learn something new. Someone refuses to use a computer when "my pad of paper is as easy." Another would "rather do it myself because teaching someone will take too long."

Doctors seem to want to solve every problem with drugs, even if there is an alternative method. Most chiropractors want to avoid drugs and surgery at almost any cost. Armies think battle-driven solutions first. Negotiators typically hate the military choice. People use the tools they know at the expense of efficiency and practicality.

Can you imagine refusing to use a computer or email? Or a cell phone? Yet, even the best sales leaders once frowned upon the use of computers, email, and mobile phones. Even today, we see salespeople refusing to use the newest tool because "it's too difficult to learn and use." In sales and management, this attitude will cost you money. Take the time to learn to use every tool and become as proficient as possible in their use.

Here are a few examples of tools that every salesperson needs to be proficient in using:

1. Customer Relationship Management Software (if your company doesn't use one, get one yourself!)
2. Email (print it on your business card)
3. Social Media (Facebook, Twitter, Instagram, etc.)
4. Cell phone (print the number on your business card)
5. LinkedIn (If you don't have a LinkedIn account, take five minutes to set one up)
6. Calendar (Microsoft Outlook, Google Calendar, Apple Messenger, etc.)
7. Word Processor (Microsoft Word, Google Docs, Apple Pages, etc.)
8. Spreadsheet (Microsoft Excel, Google Sheets, Apple Numbers, etc.)

There are plenty of other tools that are essential for sales success. Learn each one so that you can use it without fail. Never let not knowing be the excuse for not using the right tool.

Rule 22 - You Can't Please Everyone

"If you want to make everyone happy, don't be a leader. Sell ice cream." ~ Eric Geiger

---

Have you realized that there are some people you can't please? No matter what you do or what you try or how nice you are to them, you can't please everybody.

If you can honestly say you did your absolute best, that's all you can do. Some people will never be happy.

People see those who try to please everyone as weak or manipulative. In today's everyone-is-connected-to-everyone markets, don't assume that someone you have never spoken to has not already heard about you.

Jimmy (not his real name) worked with me when I sold cars. He knew sports better than anyone, especially college football. He also knew that, if he could relate to his customers, he might make more sales. So, he decided that he would discover their favorite team and show them that he was that team's biggest fan.

Jimmy knew stats and watched games. If a customer liked Michigan, Jimmy bled Maize and Blue. If they were a Michigan State fan, he was suddenly all "Go Green!" (Did I hear you say, "Go White?") He thought this gave him an edge. It worked with some customers, but he was not being genuine.

One time, Jimmy had a Michigan mouse pad on his desk when a Michigan State fan came in. He forgot to change out the pad and began talking about State as if he never watched any other team. I saw the customer glance at the mouse pad and then at Jimmy. Jimmy never saw the quick glance, but the customer left a few minutes later and never came back. I don't think Jimmy ever knew why.

Instead of trying to please everyone, be yourself! Talk about your favorite team without putting your customer's team down. Be prepared to say no if it is the right answer. And stop seeking the approval of others.

The biggest failure in life is failing to be yourself. And the biggest rejection in life is rejecting yourself. The world doesn't need another people-pleaser; the world needs the real you.

Rule 23 - Some Will, Some Won't. Move On.

"Some people are going to say yes, and some are going to say no. So what! Out there somewhere, someone is waiting for you and your ideas. It is simply a numbers game. You have to keep asking until you get a yes." ~ Jack Canfield

---

You need to be mentally tough to be in sales. You face near constant rejection and you cannot internalize it. Learning how to deal with rejection is vital; you cannot let rejection become defeat.

We all love to hear "YES!" it's affirming. It's uplifting. Sometimes, it even gives us that "Rocky Moment" where we lift our hands in the air in victory. We anticipate the yes; we expect it, and sometimes we even predict it.

"NO," on the other hand, is definitely not exciting. In sales, we hate to hear no. No means loss, it means no payout; it means you weren't good enough to close the deal.

However, "no" does not mean someone won't be willing to reconsider in the future. Move on does not mean leave them behind. No does not mean no forever.

Selling is a numbers game. You will hear "no" many times more than "yes." You don't need to close every deal. Don't expect to close every deal. If you do, you are only taking orders; you are not selling.

Save everyone's information for future opportunities. They might realize they need the exact thing you offer. Their closest friend might need what you sell. Your company might create the new whiz-bang widget that will be the best thing since pockets. And your competition will mess up and that might drive that customer right into your arms.

Be ready, but don't get bogged down in the "no." And don't sit and wait for them. Move on to your next opportunity, quickly.

Someone out there wants to buy your product. Someone is needing your service. Move forward to find your yes. No leads to yes if you keep moving.

Get past the no; find your next yes!

Rule 24 - Sometimes - You Fail

"One of the best predictors of ultimate success in either sales or non-sales selling isn't natural talent or even industry expertise, but how you explain your failures and rejections." ~ Daniel H. Pink

Like many sales people, I can look calm, cool, and collected. But underneath, I am anything but calm. I have sales quotas, expectations, bills to pay. And I only have so many hours in the day to make good things happen.

I guarantee this - when you are in sales, you will fail:

1. You lose deals you thought you had won.
2. You say something stupid.
3. You don't make your numbers - again.
4. Your prospects won't move forward.
5. Your best client went to your biggest competitor.

Everybody fails. What matters is what you do after you fail. Do you dwell on it? Or do you learn from it?

Everybody fails. It's an infallible rule of sales. You will hear "No" many times more than you will hear "Yes." Anyone who has a perfect sales career sold one thing once and never tried again. It looks impressive, but you don't make a living that way.

Sales failures become valuable learning opportunities. When you learn from your mistakes, everything changes. You stop beating yourself up. You no longer dwell on everything that went wrong, so you become more positive. And you quit trying to be perfect and simply try to be better.

And you're a lot less stressed, meaning you can see clearly and move forward to the next opportunity.

If you're struggling, keep struggling. Keep learning. Push forward to the next opportunity. Make your failures the pavement to your biggest success!

Remember - if you don't learn from your mistakes, you're bound to repeat them.

Final Rule – Find a True Companion

"And the Lord God said, 'It isn't good for man to be alone; I will make a companion for him, a helper suited to his needs.'" ~ Genesis 2:18 (TLB)

One final rule for you, and this is the most important rule.

Find that person who can be your true companion. Rely on them, share with them. Be open and honest, share everything with them and help them as much as they help you. Never let them go and never take them for granted.

Have you ever been to an amusement park alone? It's not much fun, is it? The rides aren't nearly as exciting, and the crowds are much more irritating. You need your closest, bestest friend to really enjoy an amusement park.

Sales is a tough job. It is a roller coaster that is more thrilling that any ride. It has exhilarating ups and gut-wrenching downs. Deals throw you for a loop; they always zig when you thought they were going to zag. And when you think the ride is over, the next deal comes along and the whole thing starts all over again.

The best sales people have a close companion. They are the person with whom you can enjoy the ups and downs and spins and all the other crazy stuff. For me, that companion is Kathryn.

Kathryn is my biggest fan when everything goes well, and she is my rock when the winds howl and the waves crash and the roosters crow and the cows are spinning in the field. She knows when to listen and when to help me fix it. And she never lets me wallow in self-pity for very long.

You have chosen a crazy, unpredictable, unforgiving life. Pour yourself into your career with passion and the willingness to do whatever it takes. A career in sales will reward you with wealth and opportunity and achieved dreams.

Pour yourself into your relationship with your companion in the same way. Your accomplishments will be greater and much more fulfilling. Sharing your life with someone makes you vulnerable, but the risk is so much greater than the reward!

Take the risk. Find your companion and live your life with them. Never let them go.

About the Author

David Dykstra has been selling for over 20 years. His sales career started while he was a corporate trainer and he fell backward into his first deal. After closing that first sale of over $250,000, he was hooked.

From phone sales to selling cars to leading sales teams, David lives the Rules that he writes about every day. His latest book, **Sales Rules!**, is a look at David's proven code for becoming the best salesperson possible.

David studied Entrepreneurship and International Business at Cornerstone University in Grand Rapids, MI, graduating at the top of his class with his MBA. He lives in the Grand Rapids area with his wife and true companion, Kathryn.

You can visit his website at *www.DavidBDykstra.com*.